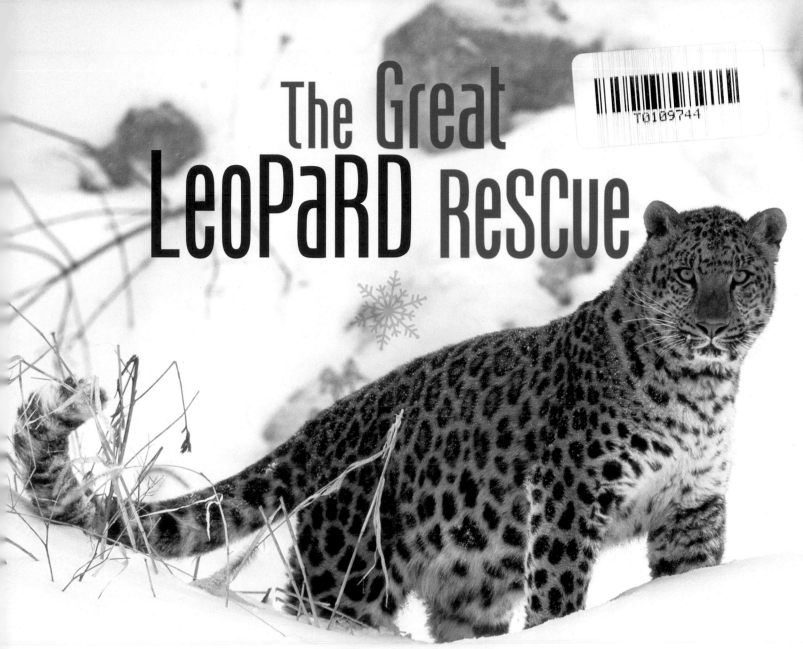

The Great LeoPaRD ReSCue

Saving the **Amur** Leopards

Sandra Markle

M Millbrook Press • Minneapolis

For dear friends Carl and Deborah Marino

Acknowledgments: The author would like to thank the following people for sharing their enthusiasm and expertise: Irina Burtseva, Deputy Director, Phoenix Fund; Darron Collins, Director of WWF–United States' Amur-Heilong Program; Jo Cook, Zoological Society of London, International Studbook Keeper; Dr. Linda Kerley and Dr. Mikhail Borisenko, Lazovsky Nature Reserve experts and Detection Dog trainers; Dr. John Lewis, Director, Wildlife Vets International; Dr. Dale Miquelle, Director of Wildlife Conservation Society–Russia; Olivia Walter, Development Manager, Wildlife Vets International. A special thank-you to Skip Jeffery for his loving support during the creative process.

First paperback edition published in 2024.

Millbrook Press™
An imprint of Lerner Publishing Group, Inc.
241 First Avenue North
Minneapolis, MN 55401 USA

For reading levels and more information, look up this title at www.lernerbooks.com.

Main body text set in Metro Office. Typeface provided by Linotype AG.

Library of Congress Cataloging-in-Publication Data

Names: Markle, Sandra, author.
Title: The great leopard rescue : saving the Amur leopards / by Sandra Markle.
Description: Minneapolis : Millbrook Press, [2017] | Audience: Ages 9–12. | Audience: Grades 4 to 6. | Includes bibliographical references and index.
Identifiers: LCCN 2015044387 (print) | LCCN 2015051353 (ebook) | ISBN 9781467792479 (lb : alk. paper) | ISBN 9781467797559 (eb pdf)
Subjects: LCSH: Leopard—Amur River Valley (China and Russia)—Juvenile literature. | Wildlife rescue—Amur River Valley (China and Russia)—Juvenile literature. | Wildlife conservation—Amur River Valley (China and Russia)—Juvenile literature.
Classification: LCC QL737.C23 M27236 2017 (print) | LCC QL737.C23 (ebook) | DDC 599.75/54—dc23

LC record available at http://lccn.loc.gov/2015044387

ISBN 979-8-7656-4328-0 (pbk.)

Manufactured in the United States of America
2-1010182-20004-11/9/2023

TABLE OF CONTENTS

DANGER!

In the fading light of an autumn day, a young male Amur leopard picks his way over a rocky ridge and sets off on his nighttime hunt. Earlier, in the morning, he caught a hare before finding a den to sleep in. But one hare isn't enough daily food for a cat nearly twice as big as a German shepherd. So, awake again, he's hungry and hunting. When his keen nose picks up the scent of blood, he tracks it.

A wounded animal would be an easy kill. But this one is another leopard's prey. With a throaty growl, the rival warns the young male to stay away. He moves on and keeps hunting.

Able to drag prey three times its weight, this leopard dragged a wild goat to a place where it could defend its meal.

A male Amur leopard's home range may cover more than 150 square miles (388 square kilometers).

As a cub, he'd spent two years shadowing his mother and learning to hunt. During the following winter, he hunted with his brother and sister in their mother's home range (the area normally traveled while hunting). They searched for prey on familiar ground and helped one another get enough to eat. But adult Amur leopards hunt alone, so in the spring, the trio split up.

All summer long, the young male wandered farther from his mother's home range. At last, he found a range of his own. Though he sometimes crosses paths with rivals and potential mates, this part of the forest is his home.

Now, he takes a path he's traveled many times. But before he picks up the scent of more prey, the wind shifts, bringing the nose-stinging smell of smoke.

Beyond the stream he's crossing, sparks dance in the air. Flames crawl through tall grass and into the dead leaves littering the forest floor. If this fire spreads upward into the trees, the entire forest could soon be ablaze. The leopard leaps over a burning patch of grass and runs for his life.

He has to survive. The wild Amur leopard population can't lose even one more big cat.

ON THE BRINK

According to studies from the World Wildlife Fund, Amur leopards are the rarest big cats on Earth. These majestic predators live primarily in the far eastern part of Russia. Experts believe a few more live in northeastern China and possibly even in South Korea.

Males and females need enough open land so their hunting ranges can overlap. This ensures they can find mates to produce young.

Amur leopards weren't always so rare. In the 1950s, scientists estimated there were about twenty-four hundred wild Amur leopards in Russia, which was then part of the Soviet Union (a union of fifteen republics). That number, based on sightings and tracks in the snow, was a healthy population for a cat that lives in a very limited part of the world. But since then, the number of wild Amur leopards recorded has dropped to about fifty. With such a small population, they are greatly at risk of becoming extinct—gone forever.

How did the situation become so desperate for Amur leopards? What upset the balance for these powerful cats?

An Amur leopard's paws and claws help it walk easily on snow and ice.

One clear reason for the leopards' decline is the loss of their forest habitat. Amur leopards live in a type of high-altitude forest known as boreal forest, or taiga. The landscape and climate make it their ideal home. This kind of forest once stretched across the far eastern corner of Russia. Because of the cold weather and rugged land, for centuries the taiga remained largely untouched by logging or other industries. Logging took place on a small scale, but it was so difficult in the taiga that only the biggest, best-quality trees were cut and floated down rivers to sawmills.

In the 1950s, heavy-duty machines were developed that allowed new access to the taiga. This new technology allowed loggers to clear-cut large areas and haul out the logs on trucks. After the land was cleared, people could mine the area for valuable minerals, such as coal. Miners scraped open the land, sometimes digging giant pits. That changed the land so much that trees couldn't grow back. Amur leopards lost much of their forest home in far eastern Russia.

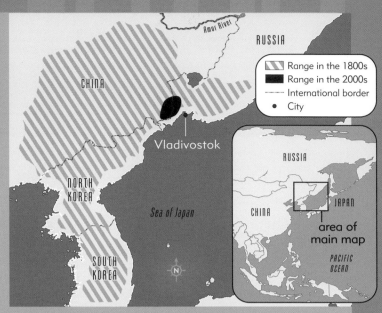

This map shows how the range of Amur leopards has shrunk over time.

Trees from the leopards' habitat in Russia were cut down and transported to be used for lumber.

Why Do Leopards Need the Taiga?

The taiga's natural features make it an excellent home for Amur leopards. It has the perfect mix of tree-covered areas with high, rocky ridges and low, open, grassy areas along rivers and lakes. The grassy areas provide plenty of food for deer, boars, and grouse, ensuring a healthy supply of these prey animals for leopards to catch. From the high ridges, the leopards can watch for prey or hide from Amur tigers (also called Siberian tigers), their main wild predators. The rocky areas also offer dens where the cats can sleep during the day after a night of hunting. And dens provide safe spaces for Amur leopards to give birth and raise cubs.

Can you find the two leopards? This pair will only stay together while mating. Then the female will raise the cubs.

Farming has harmed the taiga too. Better machinery, better fertilizers, and new hardier varieties of crops made it possible to farm areas of the taiga that were previously left wild. To clear more land for crops, farmers cut down trees. And they often cleared crop fields for replanting the next year by setting the fields on fire. Those fires sometimes spread into the nearby forest.

Combines harvest winter wheat in Russia.

By the 1970s, what remained of the wild leopard population had been divided among three fragments of forest. But the destruction of the leopards' habitat wasn't the only reason the wild Amur leopard population was shrinking.

Since ancient times, people have hunted these big cats as trophies. Russia banned leopard hunting in the 1950s, but people continued to kill the leopards. Poachers (illegal hunters) were rarely caught. If they were caught, they were fined. However, the fine was usually only a small fee.

Even legal hunting of deer and boar in the taiga threatened the leopards' survival. The big cats need a good supply of those large prey animals to live.

With so many threats to wild Amur leopards, their population crashed.

To thrive, an adult Amur leopard needs to catch and eat large prey, like roe deer, about every fifteen days.

TIME FOR ACTION

By the mid-1980s, hunting and the loss of the taiga had taken a huge toll. Leopards had completely disappeared from two of the three remaining forest areas where they'd lived. Only one forest continued to support any Amur leopards. Conservation efforts intensified to help stop poaching, protect the big cats' prey, and safeguard their habitat. Experts were doing all they could to help that one remaining group of leopards survive in the wild.

Zoos around the world joined the effort in the 1990s to keep Amur leopards from becoming extinct. By this point, new leopards were brought in only from other zoos, while in the past, they had been captured in the wild. Now zoos could help visitors learn about and appreciate these rare cats.

They also began a carefully controlled breeding program. By moving cats from zoo to zoo and keeping breeding records, they reduced the risk of inbreeding (family members mating). That prevented passing on certain inherited problems such as a short tail, which can cause balance problems, or being unable to have babies. Those issues could make the species less likely to survive.

Mother leopards give birth to as many as four cubs at a time. Litters of two or three are most common.

In the 1990s, scientists also wanted to better understand wild Amur leopards in order to protect them. So they put radio collars on some of the big cats.

Radio collars let scientists learn how Amur leopards roam as they move around in their habitat. Scientists could collect information from the collars, even during fierce winter weather and in the dark—when it had been difficult to observe the cats. They finally learned where Amur leopards travel during each season, how far the cats usually go in a day, and how large a range they occupy. Radio collar data from young cats revealed how far a cat went before claiming a home range.

The bulge on this leopard's collar is the transmitter, which sends out information about its location.

Spying on Leopards

A radio collar is fitted with a transmitter. Together with the battery and transmitting canister, a collar weighs about 15 ounces (415 grams). Modern collars use a GPS satellite–linked system, the same system smartphones use. This identifies the cat's location, correct to within about 30 feet (10 meters). That information is collected a number of times each day and is transmitted in batches by satellite once a day to a computer.

To put a radio collar on a leopard, scientists need to dart and tranquilize a cat and put a collar on while it's asleep.

In 2000 international groups working to protect Amur leopards and Amur tigers formed the Amur Leopard and Tiger Alliance (ALTA). The group organized an antipoaching team, which patrolled the leopards' habitat to arrest illegal hunters and set up roadblocks to collect any illegal firearms. The group also started working with local farmers. Farmers sometimes kill big cats to protect their livestock from becoming prey, so ALTA educates them about the rare cats and pays them for any animals killed by leopards. That has helped reduce leopard deaths in farmed areas.

ALTA patrols keep watch for poachers. ALTA also works to help local people value Amur leopards through school programs, annual art contests, and festivals.

Big paws help this cat to be sure-footed in the rugged taiga. And its long tail is perfect for helping it stay balanced.

But even such a combined effort wasn't enough. The 2007 survey of the wild Amur leopard population reported the lowest number yet. Only about thirty remained in the taiga. Clearly, the wild cats were still in danger.

In 2012 the Russian government joined the fight to protect Amur leopards. The country enacted stricter laws to stop poaching, and it finally gave the leopards a safe home—Land of the Leopard National Park, a park created especially for them.

The Land of the Leopard National Park covers about 647,000 acres (261,832 hectares), about the size of the state of Rhode Island. People can visit the park, but it's illegal to farm, hunt, mine, or harvest lumber on the parkland.

With the protected park established, the number of Amur leopards increased slightly in new surveys following the 2007 all-time low. But scientists around the world remained worried. A catastrophe such as a disease could still wipe them all out.

"Clearly what was needed," said Dale Miquelle, director of the Wildlife Conservation Society in Russia, "was a spare wild Amur leopard population." Experts agreed that a second group of wild Amur leopards, living in a separate area, would be the best protection against the wild cats becoming extinct. A disease or a disaster in the Land of the Leopard National Park would not affect the separate group of leopards, and an additional group of breeding adults would help grow the total wild population faster.

Dale Miquelle measures the paw print of an Amur tiger as part of his research on big cats in the region.

But how could people help create a new population of these wild cats?
Where would the Amur leopards come from? And where would they live?

PREPARING FOR PIONEERS

To launch this new, spare leopard population, scientists looked to zoo-bred leopards. Fortunately, the zoo breeding program started in the 1990s was maintaining a healthy captive population of Amur leopards. By 2015 the zoo population had grown to about two hundred worldwide.

Scientists created an innovative plan for several zoo leopards to temporarily live in a fenced-off part of the taiga in Russia and give birth to cubs. Then, once the young leopards were ready to hunt alone, they would be released into the forest. The parents would return to their zoo homes—the father shortly after mating and the mother after her job guarding and training the cubs was done.

Kaia at Marwell Zoo in the United Kingdom has proven she can raise cubs, like thirteen-week-old Kanika, without help. She could possibly be chosen to help launch the new wild Amur leopard population.

Starting the new population with zoo leopards made sense. Zoo breeding programs already kept genetic records and tested mating pairs to prevent passing on inherited problems. And beginning the program with zoo animals would avoid taking leopards from the already critically small wild population in the Land of the Leopard. However, scientists still needed to learn more about wild leopards if they were going to prepare the cubs of captive zoo cats to live wild in the taiga.

For example, how did Amur leopards react when they encountered another leopard? What health issues did they experience in the wild? And what kind of prey animals would young cats need to be able to hunt on their own?

Dogs on Duty

Scientists needed to know what prey animals the new Amur leopards were likely to need to hunt in different seasons. So they studied wild leopard scat (waste droppings) in laboratories. Specially trained dogs helped find these samples to analyze. Linda Kerley and her husband, Mikhail Borisenko, trained German shepherds and German wirehaired pointer dogs for this task. "While leopard scat is easy to spot on snow, it's nearly impossible to see among leaves on the forest floor," Linda said. But the dogs could sniff it out.

Thanks to these dogs, scientists learned that Amur leopards mainly catch and eat bigger prey, such as deer, during the winter. In warmer seasons, they usually eat smaller game, including hare, mice, and birds.

This German shepherd, named Panda, was a champ at sniffing out Amur leopard scat.

To help scientists better understand wild Amur leopard behavior, the Russian Academy of Sciences partnered with the World Conservation Society–Russia to place hundreds of camera traps throughout the Land of the Leopard. Camera traps aren't actually traps but cameras with motion-sensor triggers. So when a leopard (or other animal) walks past a camera, the movement triggers the camera to take a photo or a video. Each leopard's spot pattern is unique, so scientists look at their spots to tell individual leopards apart in the photos.

A scientist attaches a camera trap to a tree in the taiga. Digital images from the traps are saved to flash drives that can be picked up later or transmitted to computers in science labs.

In 2012 scientists in China also began using camera traps to study tigers and leopards on Chinese land connected to the Land of the Leopard National Park. They learned that fewer than a dozen Amur leopards were in that area. In 2015, for the first time, Russian and Chinese scientists compared data from camera traps in each country, launching a joint partnership to save the critically endangered cats.

Camera traps snap photos of wild leopard behavior, which is often similar to that of other, smaller cats. This camera caught a cat rolling on the ground and scratching its head against a tree.

Scientists also worked to find out what could affect the health of the reintroduced leopards in a forest home. First, veterinarians studied captive Amur leopards living in zoos. John Lewis, a veterinarian who leads Wildlife Vets International, examined fifty leopards and read reports on others to understand what health issues they faced.

Next, Lewis and his team of wildlife vets went in search of wild leopards to study more closely. Where camera traps showed a lot of wild leopard activity, the team set harmless foot snares. Over time, the vets caught and tranquilized eight leopards so they could examine them.

Amur leopard cub Lischinka gets a checkup at the Audubon Zoo in New Orleans, Louisiana.

Lewis and his team weighed and measured each leopard. They checked each animal's heart for murmurs (irregular blood flow sounds as the heart beats). They also checked for external parasites and collected blood and tissue samples. Back in the laboratory, scientists checked these samples for internal parasites and diseases, such as feline leukemia, which causes blood disorders, or feline calicivirus, a disease that causes respiratory problems.

Lewis reported that the wild leopards they studied, like the zoo leopards, were in good health. That indicated a new population could fare well in the wild.

Lewis's team did find that some Amur tigers had become infected with and died from canine distemper—a serious virus that can spread from domestic dogs to wild animals. So ALTA, with other conservation groups in Russia, launched an effort in the new leopard population's future home. The goal was to vaccinate all dogs against this disease. While that won't eliminate every possibly infected animal, it will greatly reduce the risk for Amur leopards and tigers alike.

John Lewis checks an instrument clamped to a cat's tongue to monitor the leopard's heart rate during the exam.

Bringing Up Baby

A female Amur leopard is always a solo mother. After carrying her babies for about three months, she finds a den and gives birth. She has one to four cubs in a litter. Each baby weighs a little more than 1 pound (0.5 kilograms). The cubs' eyes are shut, and they need to nurse often. So the mother leopard only hunts close to the den.

By the time the cubs are eight weeks old, they're exploring outside. Then the mother travels farther for food and brings home meat for the cubs. Later, they tag along and shadow her every move to learn to hunt. They will continue to nurse for about six months, and they'll need the mother's protection and training for about two years. Only then are they ready to face life in the forest alone.

SPARE HAVEN

Once scientists better understood wild Amur leopards and how they behave in their native habitat, it was time to find a home for the new population. An international team of scientists worked with Russian government officials to select a site among the remaining areas of taiga. In 2015 they chose a 467 square-mile (1,210 sq. km) area called Lazovsky Zapovednik. A *zapovednik* is land set aside for wildlife, off-limits to visitors except scientists and patrols to stop poachers and fight forest fires. Lazovsky had been home to Amur leopards before intensive hunting wiped them out, so scientists thought it would be an excellent fit for a new leopard habitat.

Lazovsky Zapovednik is far enough from the current area of wild leopards that the new leopard population there won't mix with the existing population, avoiding the spread of diseases or genetic problems.

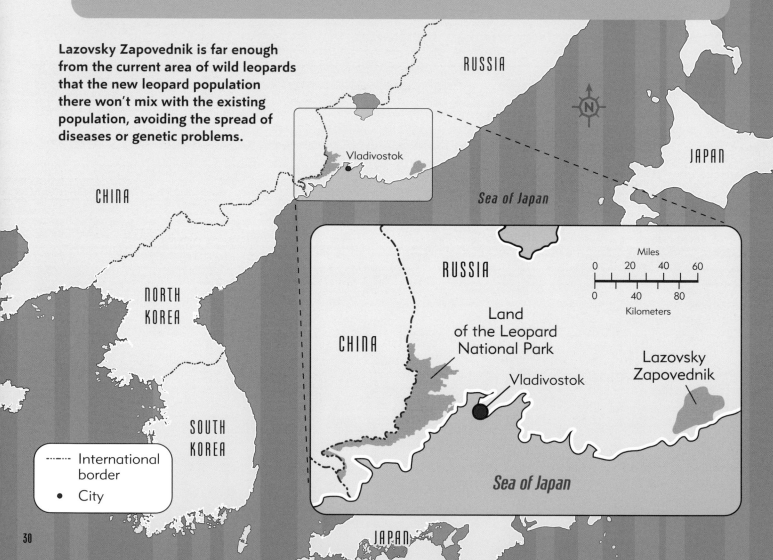

RUSSIA

Vladivostok

CHINA

Sea of Japan

JAPAN

NORTH KOREA

SOUTH KOREA

Miles
0   20   40   60

0   40   80
Kilometers

RUSSIA

Land of the Leopard National Park

CHINA

Vladivostok

Lazovsky Zapovednik

Sea of Japan

JAPAN

----- International border
• City

In fact, Lazovsky is more suited to these big cats now than in the past. According to Miquelle, of the Wildlife Conservation Society, "Climate change in this area over the past forty years has definitely favored the leopards." Like many parts of the world, this corner of Russia has seen its climate shift over time. Historically, the most northern parts of the Lazovsky area had winter snows too deep for the leopards to hunt easily. But in recent years, the entire Lazovsky area has been drier and received less snow.

Thanks to keen hearing and eyes able to see in dim light, Amur leopards are successful nighttime hunters.

INTO THE WILD

With the site chosen, the next step in the reintroduction program is building breeding enclosures for each of two pairs of leopards. These pairs will be the parents of the cubs that will grow up to live wild and free in the taiga.

Beginning in 2016, two separate parts of the Lazovsky Zapovednik are being fenced off—one for each of the leopard pairs.

Cubs must learn to be good climbers in the forest! An adult can leap about 20 feet (6 m) horizontally and 10 feet (3 m) vertically.

Each enclosure will be at least 328 feet (100 m) long. The cats need that much room to chase down prey. The width of each enclosed area will depend on the terrain. Each enclosed site will be carefully chosen to include key features for wild leopards: a rocky area for denning, a forested area for hunting, and a stream for drinking.

The fence around each enclosure needs to hold these big cats in while keeping Amur tigers and poachers out. Because big cats are good jumpers, the fence must be 16 feet (4.8 m) high and electrified.

Each fenced-off area will include a river or stream.

33

The enclosure will be shaped like a figure eight, with a gate in the middle as well as at either end. That way one or more of the big cats can be trapped in one half as needed, such as when a male is being removed after mating or while a truck releases live prey so cubs can learn to hunt. Cameras around the enclosure will let people watch the cats, but great care will be taken to keep the cats from getting accustomed to people.

The leopard's fur is longer and lighter-colored in winter—perfect for hunting in its cold, snowy habitat.

In 2017, once everything is ready for them, the Amur leopard parents will be selected from zoos and brought to the site. When the cubs born in Lazovsky are around two years old and ready to be out on their own, the mother will be returned to her home zoo. Then the gate will be opened and the cubs will be free. That exciting moment is expected to happen in 2020.

According to Jo Cook, who coordinates ALTA programs and the Amur leopard European Endangered Species Programme (EEP), her team will keep an eye on the released cubs. Those that aren't able to hunt well enough to survive on their own will be sent to live in a zoo, she explained. But she is optimistic. "The young that succeed," she said, "will be the founders of the new wild Amur leopard population."

Beware of Tigers

Amur tigers live in the same areas where Amur leopards roam. Tigers are the world's biggest cats—larger predators than Amur leopards. Amur tigers also outnumber Amur leopards, with a wild population of about five hundred.

However, adult leopards aren't usually at risk of a tiger attack. That's partly because these big cats use the habitat differently. Leopards usually keep to high ridges to hunt and to watch out for tigers. Tigers mainly hunt on lower, flatter terrain. Learning to hunt alongside their mothers, young Amur leopards also grow up knowing to avoid tigers.

A key question for the leopard reintroduction program is how to train the first generation of cubs to avoid tigers. Scientists plan to temporarily put special collars on the cubs and then bring a stuffed, life-sized toy tiger into the enclosure. Anytime the cubs get close to it, they'll receive a mild shock. Later, the scientists will introduce tiger scat, and the cubs will be shocked if they approach it. Program leaders hope this training will teach the leopards to avoid even the smell of tigers.

Male Amur tigers may grow to be 10 feet (3 m) long and weigh 700 pounds (about 318 kg).

PROTECTING THE PRESENT

Back in the Land of the Leopard forest, the young male leopard is running for his life, away from the spreading fire. Luckily, he is being watched over. The Phoenix Fund, part of ALTA, is always on the lookout for fires in the Land of the Leopard. Phoenix Fund staff keep watch from tall towers, send out ground patrols, and scan large remote areas with unmanned aerial vehicles (UAVs). One of these remote-controlled UAVs has sent back images of a grass fire. It's the fire creeping through the leaf litter in the young male leopard's home range.

This Phoenix Fund team watches as a remote-controlled UAV carrying mini-cameras takes off to patrol nearby areas.

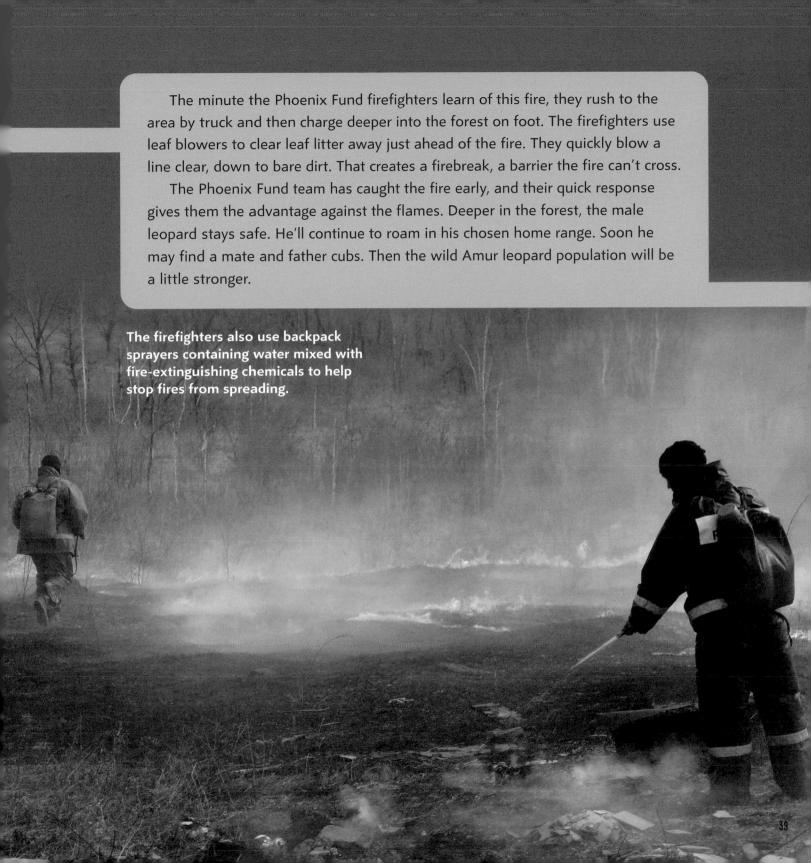

The minute the Phoenix Fund firefighters learn of this fire, they rush to the area by truck and then charge deeper into the forest on foot. The firefighters use leaf blowers to clear leaf litter away just ahead of the fire. They quickly blow a line clear, down to bare dirt. That creates a firebreak, a barrier the fire can't cross.

The Phoenix Fund team has caught the fire early, and their quick response gives them the advantage against the flames. Deeper in the forest, the male leopard stays safe. He'll continue to roam in his chosen home range. Soon he may find a mate and father cubs. Then the wild Amur leopard population will be a little stronger.

The firefighters also use backpack sprayers containing water mixed with fire-extinguishing chemicals to help stop fires from spreading.

For now, the best that can be done for Amur leopards in the Land of the Leopard is to continue protecting them and their habitat. But looking ahead, a second, spare population will ensure that Amur leopards continue to roam the taiga. It will also help to restore the total number of Amur leopards living in the wild. With healthier population levels and continued protection, these big cats may once again have a thriving future.

Amur leopards have powerful jaws and strong neck muscles—perfect for catching big prey.

Helping More Big Cats

Amur leopards aren't the only big cats that people are working to protect and reintroduce into habitats they once called home. One program is working on reintroducing wild Eurasian lynx to the United Kingdom. These cats prey on deer, so they may help reduce deer overpopulation in UK forests.

Other projects aim to reintroduce cheetahs into part of South Africa; bobcats to Cumberland Island, Georgia; and European bobcats into part of Bavaria. Like the ongoing effort to help Amur leopards, these programs could restore balance to ecosystems, help wild cats around the world recover from shrinking populations, and ensure these species continue to have a wild future.

The lynx, a medium-sized wildcat, disappeared from the United Kingdom hundreds of years ago.

Author's Note

When I first learned how people around the world were working together to preserve Amur leopards, the world's rarest big cats, I knew it was a story I had to share. At the time I started my research, the entire wild population numbered just thirty. I'd look at groups of people, count to thirty, and think, "Wow! That's all there are."

Then, each time I interviewed an expert studying Amur leopards or working to save them, the story grew bigger, and I had to dig deeper. Most exciting to me was learning about the reintroduction program. This wasn't just turning animals loose in the wild—cubs of zoo cats would be born in the taiga. These offspring of zoo cats, who'd been tended and captives their whole lives, would grow up to live totally free in their wild home.

I'm sharing this story at the very beginning of the reintroduction program. I'm excited about what it means for the future of the wild Amur leopard population, and I'll continue to follow its progress and stay in touch with the scientists I've connected with through my research. To follow along, you can check for the latest information on the ALTA website (http://www.altaconservation.org/).

I'll be eager to see the program develop, continuing to hope that the future of the Amur leopard population is *wildly* successful!

Did You Know?

Amur leopards can run as fast as 37 miles (59 km) per hour in short bursts. And they're not only good runners and jumpers, these cats are also good swimmers.

The leopard's fur is only about 1 inch (2.5 centimeters) long in summer but more than 2 inches (5 cm) long in the winter. Its winter coat is also lighter in color. That way it stays warm and blends in better while hunting in its snowy habitat.

Leopards regularly mark their home range with their urine, feces, and claw marks.

Amur leopard females don't breed until they are three or four years old. Then they spend two years raising each litter. So even though these cats may live to be fifteen years old in the wild, each female only produces a small number of young in her lifetime.

Amur leopards are named after the Amur River that forms part of the border between the Russian Far East and northeastern China.

Timeline

1956 Amur leopard hunting is banned in Russia (then part of the Soviet Union). The wild population is thought to be about twenty-four hundred.

1970 Russia first begins monitoring Amur leopard activities.

1972–1973 A Russian wild Amur leopard population survey indicates there are fewer than forty-six leopards.

1990s Radio collars are used to track and study Amur leopard travel patterns. These collars send a radio signal that can be picked up by a stationary or mobile receiver using a directional antenna (one that can be moved around).

1996 A survey of the Amur leopard population by Russian scientists with help from Wildlife Conservation Society and World Wildlife Fund finds there are fewer than fifty wild Amur leopards.

1999 Global conservation efforts result in a proposal to set aside natural areas especially for the Amur leopards and to build up the captive population and revive the wild population.

2000 Amur Leopard and Tiger Alliance (ALTA) is formed to protect Amur tigers and Amur leopards.

2000–2006 Dogs are used to find Amur leopard scat to study big cats' seasonal diet.

2007 The wild Amur leopard population is thought to be about thirty.

2010 Russian organizations, along with WWF, WCS, the Phoenix Fund, Wildlife Vets International, and others begin planning for a second, separate wild population.

2011 Scientists begin studying Amur leopard movements using radio collars with GPS tracking.

2012 Land of the Leopard National Park is set aside as a reserve especially for Amur leopards.

2015 A survey using camera traps shows a population increase to about fifty-seven leopards in Russia and almost a dozen more in China. In addition, plans for a reintroduction program are set in motion, with Lazovsky Zapovednik as the chosen site for the second population.

2016 Construction of breeding and release enclosures is scheduled to begin in Lazovsky Zapovednik.

What is one thing you would like to be able to add to this timeline in the future?

Glossary

camera trap: a weather-resistant camera with motion-sensor trigger

den: a safe shelter for leopards, where females give birth to their young

ecosystem: a community of animals that interact within a natural environment

extinct: wiped out, no longer having any living members

habitat: the natural home environment of a plant or animal

home range: an area over which an animal normally travels in search of prey or a mate

inbreeding: mating among family members, which may occur when small population groups occupy limited areas. Inbreeding is associated with a higher risk of disease or genetic problems being passed on from parents to offspring.

parasite: an animal or plant that lives in or on another, getting food and protection from its host

poachers: hunters who try to capture or kill animals illegally

predator: an animal that hunts and eats other living things in order to live

prey: an animal that is hunted and eaten for food by another animal

radio collar: a collar with a transmitter that can send out information about an animal's location

scat: an animal's waste droppings

species: one kind of living thing

tranquilize: to use a drug to put an animal to sleep temporarily. The drug is often given by a syringe or dart.

zapovednik: an area of land in Russia that's protected and kept wild

Source Notes

20 Dale Miquelle, telephone interview with the author, October 20, 2014.

24 Linda Kerley, telephone interview with the author, March 2, 2015.

31 Miquelle, interview.

35 Jo Cook, telephone interview with the author, October 23, 2014.

Find Out More

Check out these books and websites to discover even more:

Amur Leopard Cubs
https://www.youtube.com/watch?v=zSOB8SdgdXQ
In this video from ALTA, see how young Amur leopard cubs play with one another—and their mama—at the Wildlife Heritage Foundation in Ashford in the United Kingdom.

BBC One—Planet Earth, Amur Leopards
http://www.bbc.co.uk/programmes/p00382tn
Watch rare footage of a wild Amur leopard and her cub in their home forest in this clip from the BBC.

Grindley, Sally. *Paw Prints in the Snow*. New York: Bloomsbury, 2012.
Enjoy a fictional story set in the Lazovsky Zapovednik that's packed with real-life action and facts about the big cats and other wildlife living there.

Hirsch, Rebecca E. *Siberian Tigers: Camouflaged Hunting Mammals*. Minneapolis: Lerner Publications, 2015.
Investigate Siberian tigers, also known as Amur tigers, one of the Amur leopard's main competitors in the wild.

Joubert, Beverly, and Dereck Joubert. *Face to Face with Leopards*. Washington, DC: National Geographic, 2009.
What's it like to have a wild leopard walk right up to you? Find out in this first-person story, which takes an up-close look at the lives of leopards in Botswana.

Kalman, Bobbie, and Hadley Dyer. *Endangered Leopards*. New York: Crabtree, 2005.
Compare eight kinds of leopards. How are Amur leopards like the others?

Sunquist, Fiona, and Mel Sunquist. *The Wild Cat Book*. Chicago: University of Chicago Press, 2014.
Want to know more about leopards, tigers, lions, cheetahs, jaguars, and other wild felines? This giant book explores thirty-seven cat species, so you can be an expert on them all.

Index

Photo Acknowledgments

The images in this book are used with the permission of: Thomas Kitchin & Victoria Hurst/NHPA/Photoshot/Newscom, p. 1; © Yuri Smityuk/TASS/Getty Images, p. 4; © Barrie Britton/Minden Pictures, p. 5; © Nikolai Zinovyev, pp. 6–7; © TASS/ITAR-TASS Photo/Corbis, p. 7 (right); © Tom and Pat Leeson, pp. 8, 40; © Yuri Shibnev/Minden Pictures, pp. 9, 11, 16, 17, 32–33; © Laura Westlund/Independent Picture Service, pp. 10 (top), 30; © Environment Images/UIG/Getty Images, p. 10 (bottom); © Yevgeny Kurskov/Corbis, p. 12; © Igor Shpilenok/Minden Pictures, p. 13; © Ed Godden/ Digital Camera Magazine/Getty Images, pp. 14–15; © Amur Leopard and Tiger Alliance (ALTA), p. 18; © Tom Brakefield/ Corbis, p. 19; © MICHAEL NICHOLS/National Geographic Stock, p. 20; © Anna Yu/E+/Getty Images, p. 21; Tony Gardner Photography/Rex USA, pp. 22–23; © Linda Kerley/Zoological Society of London, p. 24; © Jonathan C. Slaght, Ph.D/ Wildlife Conservation Society Russia Program, p. 25; © SEBASTIEN BOZON/AFP/Getty Images, p. 25; Europics/Newscom, p. 26 (all); AP Photo/Bill Haber, p. 27; © Dr John Goodrich/Wildlife Vets International, p. 28; © Dale Miquelle/Wildlife Conservation Society, p. 31; © SEBASTIEN BOZON/AFP/Getty Images, p. 32 (left); © Yuri Smityuk/TASS/Getty Images, pp. 34–35; © 145/Donald A Higgs/Ocean/Corbis, pp. 36–37; © Phoenix Fund, p. 38; © TASS/ITAR-TASS Photo/Corbis, p. 39; © Frank Sommariva/imageBROKER/Corbis, p. 41; AP Photo/Tom Uhlman, p. 43; REUTERS/Ilya Naymushin, p. 46.

Front cover: © Tom and Pat Leeson.

Back cover: © iStockphoto.com/Oleg_Rubik.